Wilbur & Orville Wright

THE FLIGHT TO ADVENTURE

Wilbur & Orville Wright

THE FLIGHT TO ADVENTURE

By Louis Sabin and JoAnn Early Macken
Illustrated by John Lawn

SCHOLASTIC INC.
New York   Toronto   London   Auckland   Sydney
Mexico City   New Delhi   Hong Kong   Buenos Aires

ISBN 0-439-88007-6

12 11 10 9 8 7 6 5 4 3 2   6 7 8 9 10 11/0

Printed in the U.S.A.
First printing, September 2006

CONTENTS

CHAPTER 1:
A New Baby Brother

August 19, 1871, was a sunny, steamy day in Dayton, Ohio. The three Wright brothers sprawled under a tall tree in front of the white frame house at 7 Hawthorn Street. It was too hot to play ball or tag, too hot to do much of anything. Besides, something important was happening in the house, and the boys wanted to stay nearby.

The screen door swung open, and their father, Milton Wright, stepped out onto the wide front porch. "You can come in now, boys," he said, smiling. "There's a fine baby brother waiting to meet you."

Ten-year-old Reuchlin, eight-year-old Lorin, and four-year-old Wilbur Wright rushed up the porch steps into the house. Without stopping, they dashed upstairs to the second floor and into their parents' bedroom.

Their mother, Susan Wright, was sitting up in bed, holding the newborn baby. "Children," she said, "I'd like you to meet Orville." Then, smiling at the baby in her arms, she added, "Orville, here are your three big brothers."

The baby yawned and closed his eyes.

The three boys, standing next to the bed, laughed loudly. Wilbur moved closer. "When will he be big enough to play with me?" he asked. "Reuchlin and Lorin have each other, so Orville has to be my best friend."

Mr. Wright picked up Wilbur and hugged him. "Soon enough, son," he told the four-year-old. "And I know you two will be best friends. Just give Orville a little time to grow."

Wilbur and Orville were close right from the start, and they stayed that way all through their lives. As Wilbur wrote many years later, "From the time we were little children, my brother Orville and I lived together, played together, worked together, and, in fact, thought together. We usually owned all of our toys in common, talked over our thoughts and aspirations so that nearly everything that was

done in our lives has been the result of conversations, suggestions, and discussions between us."

CHAPTER 2:
A Special Toy

When Orville was five years old, he was given a special kind of toy called a gyroscopic top. It had two wheels, one inside the other. The outside wheel could spin up and down while the inside one spun from side to side. The top had such perfect balance that it could keep spinning even when it was set on the edge of a knife blade.

Orville and Wilbur played with the new toy for hours. Like all mechanical things, it fascinated the brothers. They wanted to know how the top worked. So Wilbur, who was a very good reader, went to the library. He came home with as many books as he could find about tops and gyroscopes. He read the books to Orville, and they talked about them. Although some of the science was too hard for the boys to understand, they learned.

Many times, when the boys had questions about mechanical things, they asked their mother. Susan Wright was an unusual woman for the nineteenth century. In those days, not many men and even fewer women had much education. But Mrs. Wright, like her husband, had been to college. She was especially good at mathematics and science and anything mechanical. When something around the house needed to be fixed, Mrs. Wright did the job. If she wanted to make or fix something but did not have a tool to do it, she made a tool herself. She even made a sled for Reuchlin and Lorin.

Mrs. Wright helped the boys learn how the gyroscopic top worked. Most of the time, though, she wanted them to figure things out by themselves. Mr. Wright agreed that the boys should learn as much as they could on their own. Often, when the children asked him for information, he said, "Look it up in a book. If I tell you the answer, you'll probably forget it. But if you find it yourself, you'll remember it a great deal longer. Best of all, you'll know where to find it again if you do forget. That's what books are for."

The Wright family had plenty of books right in their home. Mr. Wright kept many in his study upstairs. The living room, where the family spent hours every evening, held bookcases full of novels, fairy tales, biographies of famous men and women, history books, and two sets of encyclopedias. In those days, before the

invention of radio, television, and movies, reading was a main form of entertainment. Many evenings in the Wright home were spent listening to one of the family members read aloud from a book, newspaper, or magazine.

The Wrights also believed that their children should learn to be independent,

so every one of the young Wrights earned spending money by doing odd jobs. Orville and Wilbur were paid one penny each night for drying the dinner dishes. All of the children were paid for running errands, cleaning out the fireplaces, shoveling snow, chopping firewood—any useful job that needed to be done.

CHAPTER 3:

"Why Won't It Fly?"

In 1878, when Wilbur was eleven and Orville was seven, the family moved to Cedar Rapids, Iowa. Mr. Wright, who was a bishop in the United Brethren Church, had been given a parish in that city. Here, in their new home on Adams Street, the boys received a gift that would one day help them change the history of the world.

Mr. Wright brought the gift with him when he came home from a business trip. It was a small "flying machine" that flew like a helicopter. It was made of cork, bamboo,

and thin paper. The machine's "motor" was a rubber band that had to be twisted many times. When the rubber band couldn't be twisted anymore, the person holding the machine let go. It rose straight up, hovered for a few seconds above everyone's heads, and then floated down to the floor.

The boys nicknamed their flying toy the "Bat." They played with it day and night until it finally wore out. Instead of trying to repair the toy, they decided to build a new, improved Bat. Orville was still too young to do much of the work, but he helped Wilbur whenever he could.

Their first homemade model was bigger than the original flying machine. It was roughly made, and it didn't fly very well.

"Why won't it fly?" Orville asked his brother.

"Maybe we cut the bamboo pieces too thick," Wilbur said. "Besides, we didn't do a very careful job. It's kind of messy."

"Could we make another one? I've saved up ten cents. We can use it to buy the rubber bands," Orville said.

"Okay, Orville. I have twenty-five cents," Wilbur said. "That will be enough for the rest of the parts we need. But this time let's make a really big Bat—and fly it outside!"

The boys bought the material they needed and drew the plans. For weeks, they worked on their flying machine. Every day after school, they rushed home, did their homework, and continued to build the "Big Bat." At last, it was ready for its first flight.

One bright Saturday morning, Orville and Wilbur called the family outside to see the Big Bat fly. They set up chairs on the porch for their mother and father. Reuchlin, Lorin, and their four-year-old sister, Katherine, sat on the porch steps.

Orville held the Big Bat while Wilbur twisted the double-thick rubber band. "Ready," Wilbur said. "When I count to three, let it fly. One . . . two . . . three!"

Orville let go. For a second, the Big Bat hung in the air. Then it crashed to the ground. Both boys turned sad faces

to their family. After a moment's silence, Orville wailed, "Thirty-five cents! Think of all the ice cream we could have had."

The family burst into laughter. Mrs. Wright said, "It almost flew. Why don't you boys try again?"

"Not right now, Mother," Wilbur said. "We don't know enough about making a flying machine. Anyway, Orville and I don't have any more money."

When the brothers weren't working on one kind of machine or another, they did the things most boys did in those days. They went to the local public schools. They played baseball in the spring and summer and football in the fall. At the local pond, they swam in the summer, and ice-skated and played hockey in the winter.

The brothers' outside playtime wasn't always spent together. When Wilbur was

in junior high, his friends were eleven and twelve years old. They didn't want to have anything to do with Orville and his grade-school friends. At home, however, the brothers were still as close as ever.

CHAPTER 4:
A New Invention

In 1881, when Orville was ten and Wilbur was fourteen, the Wrights moved to Richmond, Indiana. That summer, Orville found a new hobby that took up all of his time—making and flying kites. His kites flew well because he made the frames light so they bent in the wind. He even sold some of the kites he built.

Orville earned spending money in other ways. He folded an eight-page weekly paper for a local church. Because he found the work boring, he designed and built a

device to fold the paper for him. It worked with a foot pedal. After school and on Saturdays, he pulled his wagon around the neighborhood to pick up scrap metal. He made regular trips to a chain factory to pick up leftover metal. He sold his collection at a local junk dealer's yard.

Orville had a reason for earning money. He wanted to buy the parts to build a lathe, a machine that shapes a piece of metal or wood by holding it and turning it against a cutting edge. When Orville finally saved enough money, the lathe he made was too small to be very useful.

Wilbur offered to help Orville build a bigger lathe. With a better machine, they could do all kinds of woodworking jobs. Orville loved the idea, and they set to work making the lathe right away. They built it in the barn behind the Wright house. It was powered by a foot pedal, and it worked well.

Wilbur was pleased with their success, but he had another idea. The lathe rattled and needed to be oiled all the time. Wilbur noticed that bicycles used ball bearings to make them run smoothly. Why not put ball bearings on the lathe? He decided to give it a try.

Behind the barn, Wilbur found a couple of metal rings that had been part of the harness for a horse. He didn't have steel ball bearings, so he used clay marbles.

All the youngsters in the neighborhood came to see the Wright brothers' latest invention in action. Orville sat down to work the pedal. Wilbur had a fresh piece of wood ready for shaping. Suddenly, they heard a loud noise. *Rattle! Bang! Crash!* The whole barn shook!

"Golly!" gasped one of the boys. "A couple more turns of your ball bearings, and this whole barn will fall apart.

Looks like you made a mistake this time, Wilbur."

Wilbur checked his invention and saw that it really didn't work very well. The machine had crushed the clay marbles. But why did that make the whole barn shake? The mystery was solved a few minutes later. Orville looked outside and found

his sister Katherine blown against the side of the house. A small tornado had passed through Richmond at the same time they tried out the lathe!

Later, Wilbur and Orville added a front porch to their house, complete with handsome railings and posts they had made themselves.

CHAPTER 5:
A Circus!

The next brilliant Wright idea was Orville's. It came to him while playing with Gansey Johnston, the boy who lived in the house next door. Gansey's father had an interesting hobby—taxidermy, or stuffing dead animals. The Johnstons' barn was filled with a giant grizzly bear, a black bear, several ducks, a raccoon, a beaver, and a number of other animals. Every one looked almost alive.

"Do you know what, Gansey?" Orville said. "We could have a circus using all of these animals. We could hold it right here in the barn. I know a couple of boys who can tumble and juggle, and Wilbur has a friend who rides a unicycle. We can make some money by charging admission. Do you want to be my partner?"

Gansey agreed that it was a terrific scheme. So did Harry Morrow, who wanted to get into the partnership. So the Great W. J. & M. Circus was born. The boys planned to stage a parade and a number of acts in the barn. That night, Orville told Wilbur about the great circus.

"Don't you think it's going to be wonderful?" Orville said. "We'll charge three cents for kids under three years old and five cents for everyone else. I bet we'll make a lot of money."

Wilbur thought for a moment. Then, half-joking, he said that such a grand show deserved a notice in the local newspaper, the *Richmond Evening Item*. He offered to write a description of the circus and give it to the paper. Orville and his partners loved the idea.

Wilbur's article, which was printed, used words such as "mammoth," "stupendous," and "colossal." He announced that the three partners would lead a parade on "iron horses." Harry Morrow had to leave town, but Orville and Gansey led the parade on high-wheeled bicycles. The streets were lined with people. So many showed up for the circus that they couldn't all fit in the barn.

Some of the people who paid admission were annoyed to find that it wasn't a real circus. But most just laughed and said that anyone with such a good imagination was sure to be a success. They willingly paid the few pennies to look at the stuffed animals and watch the young performers.

CHAPTER 6:
Trouble at School

When school let out in June 1884, the Wright family moved back to Dayton, Ohio. In September, when school began again, Orville went into seventh grade—but not before facing a problem. He wasn't a poor student. In fact, he was good in school. But he had been up to some mis-

chief at the Richmond school the previous
June. His teacher had sent him home and
told him to come back with his parents.
The Wrights moved before they could
meet with the teacher.

In September, Orville arrived at the
Dayton school without proof that he had
finished sixth grade. At first, the school
principal didn't want to let him into
seventh grade. Orville explained what
had happened in Richmond. He swore
he would behave himself. He promised
to work hard in all of his classes, if only

they'd give him a chance. At last, the principal agreed. He wasn't sorry. Not only was Orville an excellent student, he also finished the year with the highest arithmetic mark in the whole city of Dayton.

The move affected Wilbur's school record in a different way. He didn't have any problems at the Richmond high school. But the family move took place a few days before graduation. If Wilbur wanted his official high school diploma, he had to go back for graduation.

Wilbur felt that the piece of paper wasn't worth the trip back to Richmond. His parents said the decision was up to him. Mr. Wright added, "You went to school to learn. A diploma just tells others that you helped fill the classrooms—not that anything of value filled your head."

Finishing high school—even without a diploma—did not end Wilbur's education. Of all the Wright children, Wilbur was the one who most loved books. He was always teaching himself new subjects from library books. He also took advanced courses in Greek and mathematics at Central High School in Dayton. He even planned to go away to college—until he had a bad accident. The winter before he was to leave, he was playing shinny, an ice hockey game, and was hit in the face with a stick. He lost all his upper front teeth.

The doctor advised him to take it easy and let time heal his injuries. For several years after that, he suffered from a heart problem. He stayed home and took care of his mother, who was sick. She died in 1889.

CHAPTER 7:
Newspaper Days

Both boys continued to work with mechanical things. Orville and his friend Ed Sines set up their own printing company. They used a small printing press to put out a newspaper, called *The Midget* because the pages were tiny. They planned to sell the paper to their eighth-grade classmates, but Orville's father put an end to their plan. He saw that they hadn't filled up the last page because they thought it was too much work. He told the boys their readers would think they were lazy.

Later, the boys took on small printing jobs for Dayton businesses. They were even able to hire a neighbor to help them—for a salary of fifteen cents a week.

Most of the time, their customers paid in cash. A few didn't pay at all. One, who owed them two dollars, offered to pay them in popping corn. Orville wanted to sell the popcorn and invest the money in more printing equipment, but Ed didn't agree. He wanted to split up the popcorn and eat it. In the end, Ed kept the popcorn and Orville kept the business. Ed became an employee instead of an owner.

Orville worked for a printing company during two summer vacations. He worked long hours to learn the business. Then Wilbur helped him build a new, larger printing press. With the same kind of inventiveness their mother had shown, the boys put together a superb machine. They used wood from the woodshed, metal from junkyards, and parts of the old family buggy.

The press didn't seem to follow the rules of mechanics, and everyone was sure it wouldn't work. But it did, and very well. One day, a finely dressed man walked into the Wright brothers' printing shop and

asked to see the homemade press. He explained that he was in the printing business in another town and had heard about their invention. He looked the machine over from top to bottom, inside and out. He even lay down on the floor under the machine to watch it run. Finally, he said, "It works all right. But I still don't understand why it works."

For his last year of high school, Orville only went to school for an hour or two each day. He and Wilbur ran the printing business together after school and on weekends, putting out the *West Side News*, a weekly newspaper. Ed Sines worked for them as a reporter and advertising salesman. They also did printing jobs for local businesses.

When Orville finished high school in 1890, he and Wilbur turned the newspaper into a daily paper. They hired a new

reporter, Orville's classmate and friend. He was Paul Laurence Dunbar, who would one day be a well-known poet. On the wall of the shop, the young Dunbar wrote these words:

Orville Wright is out of sight
In the printing business.
No other mind is half so bright
As his'n is.

With too much competition from other daily papers, the newspaper was not profitable. The brothers stopped printing it after about four months. They still published a small weekly paper called *Snapshots* with news about local events.

CHAPTER 8:
The Flying Machine

In 1892, Orville and Wilbur started a new hobby—riding bicycles. Orville even became a bicycle racer for a while. Within a few months, this hobby turned into another business. The brothers put Ed Sines in charge of the printing shop, which left them free to sell and repair bicycles. They built and sold three custom models: the Van Cleve, the St. Clair, and the Wright Special.

As much as they enjoyed their successful business, the Wright brothers never

stopped thinking about flying machines. They read everything they could about ballooning, gliding, and the many kinds of flying machines that had been tried through the years. They wrote to people all over the world who shared their dream of flying.

At the same time, Orville and Wilbur began to work on their own designs for a flying machine. They used ideas they had learned from childhood on—from their experiments with the Big Bat, from kite building, and from the experience of making their own printing presses, lathes, and bicycles. They watched birds fly to see how they twisted the tips of their wings to control their balance.

In 1899, the Wright brothers built a large biplane kite, and Wilbur flew it. The kite had five-foot wings that could be moved by cords from the ground.

Next, they built a glider and shipped it in pieces to Kitty Hawk, North Carolina. Year after year, they camped out at Kitty Hawk because of the good winds in the area. After testing more than a thousand

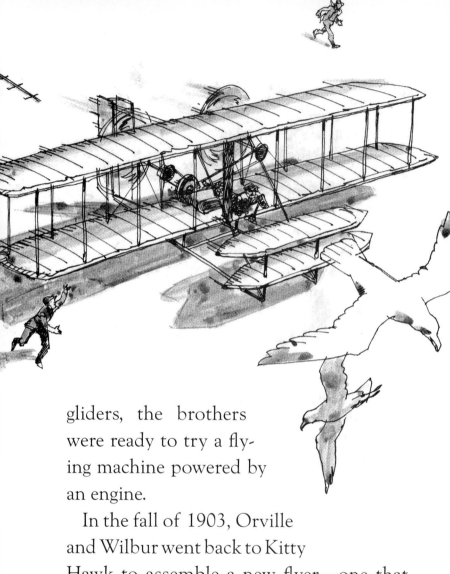

gliders, the brothers were ready to try a flying machine powered by an engine.

In the fall of 1903, Orville and Wilbur went back to Kitty Hawk to assemble a new flyer—one that could carry a person. Bad weather held them up. The machine broke on the first try. Finally, the brothers succeeded. On December 17, 1903, their power-driven, heavier-than-air machine took off!

Orville flew first. He stayed in the air about twelve seconds and traveled about one hundred twenty feet. Then Wilbur had his turn. They each had one more flight that day, and then the machine flipped over in the wind and was wrecked. But the Wright brothers had opened the door to the Age of Flight!

Orville and Wilbur continued to improve their original airplane design. Problems set them back every now and then but didn't stop them. They kept right on going—higher and farther each year.

After Wilbur died, on May 30, 1912, Orville kept designing better flying machines. His devotion to aviation ended only with his death on January 30, 1948.

The Wright brothers turned the dream of flying into a reality. Today, as we reach into space, the world owes a huge debt to the vision and creativity of Wilbur and Orville Wright.

INDEX

Look for these other exciting
EASY BIOGRAPHIES:

Abigail Adams

Elizabeth Blackwell

Marie Curie

Amelia Earhart

Thomas Edison

Albert Einstein

Helen Keller

Martin Luther King, Jr.

Abraham Lincoln

Rosa Parks

Harriet Tubman

George Washington